M000029275

HEALING FROM DIVORCE

28 Days of Prayer

Mary Lou Redding

UPPER ROOM BOOKS®

NASHVILLE

HEALING FROM DIVORCE: 28 Days of Prayer
Copyright © 2013 by Mary Lou Redding
All rights reserved.

No part of this book may be used or reproduced in any manner whatsoever without permission except in the case of brief quotations embodied in critical articles or reviews. For information, write Upper Room Books, 1908 Grand Avenue, Nashville, TN 37212.

The Upper Room website: www.upperroom.org

UPPER ROOM®, UPPER ROOM BOOKS®, and design logos are trademarks owned by The Upper Room®, a ministry of GBOD®, Nashville, Tennessee. All rights reserved.

All scripture quotations, unless otherwise indicated, are from the New Revised Standard Version Bible, copyright © 1989 National Council of the Churches of Christ in the United States of America. Used by permission. All rights reserved.

Scripture designated NIV is from the HOLY BIBLE, NEW INTERNATIONAL VERSION. NIV®. Copyright © 1973, 1978, 1984 by International Bible Society. Used by permission of Zondervan. All rights reserved.

Scripture designated KJV is from the King James Version of the Bible.

Cover image: Shutterstock.com © Skylines
Cover design: Left Coast Design, Portland, OR / www.lcoast.com

Library of Congress Cataloging-in-Publication Data
Redding, Mary Lou, 1950–
    Healing from divorce : 28 days of prayer / Mary Lou Redding.
        pages cm
    ISBN 978-0-8358-1315-0 (print)—ISBN 978-0-8358-1316-7 (mobi)—
ISBN 978-0-8358-1317-4 (epub)
1. Divorced people—Religious life. 2. Divorced people—Prayers and devotions. I. Title.
    BV4596.D58R435 2014
    242'.646--dc23
                                                2013023787
Printed in the United States of America

To the single adults

of

Brentwood United Methodist Church,

a community of

compassion, forgiveness, and healing

CONTENTS

INTRODUCTION

The title of this book may seem to imply that persons can heal from divorce in only twenty-eight days of prayer. That is not true. Healing from the pain and loss of a failed marriage comes at a different pace for each person enduring the loss, and healing takes as long as it takes. Healing is a journey, and these meditations are meant to help with *some* of the journey. Divorce represents a great loss because it is the loss of a primary relationship. According to psychologist Abraham Maslow, the needs for love and what he called "belongingness"—lasting emotional bonds with significant people—are basic human needs. Most of us cannot move beyond ourselves to care deeply and selflessly for others until these needs are met. When a marriage ends, the people divorcing lose a most significant relationship, and that presents a struggle if not a crisis.

For believers, the reality that most Christians see divorce as a failure not only in their relationship with the spouse but also in their relationship with God compounds the pain of loss. Christ's love for the church—perfect, unflagging, patient in spite of our unfaithfulness and sin—serves as the model for Christian marriage. For Christians, divorce loads spiritual issues on top of relational ones.

I felt that my divorce marked me permanently as a failure. As a church professional, I thought my personal Christian witness was damaged beyond repair and that my career was probably over. And my heart was broken. I had loved my husband. We married with hope for our future together; divorce was never part of my dream for our life. Yet our toxic relationship damaged both of us. I poured so much energy into trying to save our marriage that I had nothing left to give to God or others. So when we decided to divorce, we were choosing life—though that's probably not what it looked like from the outside. This does not mean that we took the easy way out. We took what was for us the *only* way out.

I thought my contributions to the church ended when my marriage ended. But in the years since, my most frequent place of serving and belonging within the body of Christ has been with single adults. What I thought was my biggest failure has opened the door to a new way of looking at people and at Christ's ministry of healing. Henri J. M. Nouwen wrote about "wounded healers." I've come to see that there's no other kind. We are all wounded, and we are all called to take part in what God is doing to bring healing to those around us. Divorce opened my eyes to understand God's grace not as something we earn by being good but as healing love that comes to us precisely because of our brokenness and inability to be the persons God created us to be.

These meditations do not offer answers. In fact, one of them urges those going through divorce to live the questions and even to love the questions as much as the answers. Each meditation suggests a Bible reading and quotes a Bible verse. Each one also includes a "story," along with a question or exercise for reflection. I hope those who use these meditations will take time to read the suggested Bible passages. That's the source of the deepest truth and the real power.

The meditations are aimed primarily at individuals. I intend the reflection questions and exercises to help readers apply the daily content to their specific situation. We hope this book will be a resource for individuals going through divorce. Groups can use the content by reading aloud one of the suggested daily scripture passages, summarizing the accompanying meditation, allowing silence for reflection, and then inviting responses to the reflection exercise.

You picked up this book for a reason. Maybe you've been through a divorce; maybe you've stood by people you love as they walked this difficult road. Maybe your compassionate heart urged you to read these meditations as preparation to help those in pain. Whatever your reasons, I pray that you will find God's unfailing and abundant grace made specific and real for you personally as you read.

MARY LOU REDDING
Nashville, Tennessee
Spring 2013

How to Use This Book

- Sit quietly for a minute or so before beginning each day's reading to calm your spirit.
- Read the suggested scripture passage slowly, noticing words or phrases that catch your attention. After you complete the reading, think about the passage and what in it "spoke" to you.
- Read the Bible verse quoted above the day's meditation. If it is a familiar verse, what new idea do you hear in it today? If it is a verse unfamiliar to you, consider what it says to you about God and God's grace for your situation.
- Read the day's meditation. Consider how the writer's words connect to you and your life (or not). What in the reading do you need or want to think more about?
- Pray the day's prayer, adding to it from your own life and concerns.
- Read and respond to the day's reflection question. You may want to write your responses in a journal or note-

book. Though taking time to write may seem extravagant, doing so is a gift you can give yourself. Reflection moves us from experience to meaning—but the pace of life often interferes with our finding time to take this crucial step. If you don't have time to write a full response, make a few notes and come back to writing at another time. If you do, God will use the intervening time to help you see more deeply into your life and to hear the lessons it has to teach you.

WEEK 1

....

Broken Hearts, Broken Dreams

MONDAY
Death of a dream

Read Psalm 38:9-15.

The LORD is near to the brokenhearted, and saves the crushed in spirit.

—Psalm 34:18

Susie Homemaker, Anytown, USA, died yesterday after a long and painful illness. Susie fought valiantly but in the end succumbed to the illness that had limited her for some time. She is survived by a wide circle of family and friends who will miss her greatly.

Soon after my husband and I separated, I dreamed that I was standing beside my own grave. With crushing heaviness in my chest, I looked down at the mounded earth where scattered blades of grass had begun to grow. My friend Susie stood at my side. Susie's presence in my dream was a pun (frequent in dreams and often key to understanding them). For most of my life, I had referred to my dream of having a traditional home and family as my "Susie Homemaker" ideal—a life I had desired, prayed for, and worked years to save.

Now that possibility was dead. In my dream I had been buried in a ruffled apron—a visual representation of my hopes for marriage and family. I said to my friend Susie, "But I want that apron. We have to dig up the body so I can get it."

"Are you sure you want to do that?" Susie asked. "The body has been buried for four months already. The corpse will be rotting; there will be maggots and all kinds of horrible stuff." Sighing, I agreed that retrieving the apron was a bad idea.

That dream forced me to face the fact that my marriage was dead, which allowed me to move on with my life.

Every divorce represents the death of many dreams, and every death brings grief. In the Bible, the prophet Hosea shows that he knew about the death of dreams. Hosea married Gomer as a symbol of God's faithfulness to Israel in spite of the people's faithlessness and rebellion. Hosea named their first child Jezreel, which means "God sows." Such a name symbolizes belief in life to come, in fruitfulness, in hope. But by the time the third child came, Hosea had lost hope. He named that child Loammi, which means "Not My People"—symbolizing a break in relationship and the lack of a place to belong.

With Hosea and with us, God mourns. God understands the pain of broken dreams; each one of us has frustrated God's dreams for us. In doing so, we grieve God's loving heart. As we stand by the grave of a marriage—as we sort and divide belongings, as we maneuver through the legal issues, as we struggle to find our way forward—God watches and works and walks with us. We are not alone. You are not alone. God understands the pain.

Prayer

God, my comforter, lift from my heart the heaviness of grief at this loss. Help me offer you the burdens I bear today and to believe that you will carry them for me. Amen.

Reflection — *my failure to trust Him*

Today, I place in God's care my concerns for/about. . . .

- *my children*
- *relationships*
- *my future*
- *my finances*
- *How to provide for myself*
- *my broken dreams*

TUESDAY
The circle of mourners

Read Galatians 6:1-10.

Thus says the LORD: A voice is heard in Ramah, lamentation and bitter weeping. Rachel is weeping for her children; she refuses to be comforted.

—Jeremiah 31:15

I loved my mother-in-law, and she loved me. Our divorce broke this wonderful woman's heart. Seeing her pain made me realize that I was not the only one grieving. I had married her youngest son, her baby (and we know how mothers are about their baby boys). She wanted him to be happy. She wanted for him all the things he wanted for himself—a home, children, happiness. Our divorce signaled that this was not to be, at least not in the ways we all had hoped and prayed for.

My mother-in-law was not the only one in pain. Every divorce creates a circle of grief that ripples outward from the two who are divorcing. If there are children, they grieve for the loss of the home they have known. Other family members mourn the loss or potential loss of contact with in-laws, cousins, grandchildren. Family gatherings and holidays will not be the same. The couples groups my husband and I had been a part of—our Sunday school class, our covenant/study group from church, the friends we played cards with every weekend—were saddened. Our friends, especially the closest ones, were shaken by the reality of our failure. After all, we were Christians; Christians are supposed to be able to weather any storm with God's help. But we could not save our marriage.

Beneath some of the grief in those around us lay fear—fear that their own relationships were not as secure as they had thought. Beneath some of it lay disappointment. In families facing the first divorce within their ranks, some of the grief overlays shame. "We've never had anyone divorce. We're not that kind of people." Beneath some of it is pain at seeing *our* pain, as with my mother-in-law for her son and for our future.

As we make our way through this pain, God invites us also to respect the pain of others. They need our prayers as much as we need the prayers of those who love us. We may not really want to pray for them. Deep hurt and long-standing struggles may make praying for those affected by our divorce tough. But James 5:16 tells us, "Pray for one another, so that you may be healed." As we pray for others, we open the door for our own healing to begin.

Prayer

O God, I pray today for all those who are in pain because of our divorce. Help all of us, O God, to deal gently with one another as we face the challenges that lie before us. Help us remember that each of us is one of your deeply loved children and that you desire healing and healthy relationships for us. Amen.

Reflection

Who is in pain because of this divorce? What do I ask God to do for the people within that circle?

WEDNESDAY
Breach of contract

Read Psalm 42:1-5.

> *The race is not to the swift, nor the battle to the strong, nor bread to the wise, nor riches to the intelligent, nor favor to the skillful; but time and chance happen to them all.*

—Ecclesiastes 9:11

A television ad popular a few years ago features a series of child actors making statements like these: "I want to grow up to work in a dead-end job." "I want to be underpaid and ill-appreciated." "I want to spend my life in obscurity." The ad points out that no one plans to fail. None of us grows up desiring a damaging relationship that ends with divorce.

I heard the host of a television talk show ask a young actress if she planned to marry. She blithely replied, "Probably. And if it doesn't work out, I'll just get a divorce." Most people do not share such a casual attitude toward marriage. In fact, we often look with pity or disdain at celebrities who have been married four or five or even more times and wonder why they cannot find good relationships. But believers are not immune to bad marriages. In fact, the divorce rate among evangelical believers is even higher than for the general population.

As I wrestled with the truth of my divorce, I found myself angry at God. *How could this happen to me?* I had prayed since my teen years for the person who would one day become my husband. The contract I had with God—or at least the one I assumed—did not include divorce and single parenting. I believed that God would guide me and take care of me if I prayed and followed what I thought was God's will.

My anger at God points to a struggle many of us have. We assume that if we pray and do our best, our lives will be okay and no big tragedies will come to us. Martin Luther King Jr. said in his sermon "A Knock at Midnight" that we have rewritten the Great Commission* to read, "Go ye into all the world, keep your blood pressure down, and, lo, I will make you a well-adjusted personality."**

For believers, part of the struggle in divorce comes in being forced to examine our ideas about God and God's will. Following Christ does not guarantee that we'll get what we want out of life. God promises to walk with us, yes—but sometimes our path takes us through "the valley of the shadow of death." Whether our lives embody what we envisioned and wanted or not, God can shoulder our feelings and words about where we find ourselves today.

Prayer

Dear God, I don't understand how I got to this place. It's not what I wanted for my life. Help me, O God, to find my way toward the healing you desire for me and for all involved in this pain. Amen.

Reflection

How does divorce challenge my ideas about God and God's will for me today?

---

* Matthew 28:19: "Go ye therefore, and teach all nations, baptizing them in the name of the Father, and of the Son, and of the Holy Ghost . . . and, lo, I am with you always, *even* unto the end of the world" (KJV).

**Martin Luther King Jr. "A Knock at Midnight" in *Strength to Love* (Philadelphia: Fortress Press, 1963), 57.

THURSDAY
The land called denial

Read Genesis 13:1-12.

There was strife between the herders of Abram's livestock and the herders of Lot's livestock.

—Genesis 13:7

We humans can be amazingly stubborn. Operating on emotion, we may cling to ideas and situations when reason makes it clear that circumstances need to change. Even more difficult to face, *we* may need to change. But we resist.

My marriage had been damaging and painful for years, and my husband and I had tried many remedies. We went to counseling together and separately; I prayed and fasted, bargaining with God and asking for a miracle in exchange for anything God wanted me to do. No miracle came. Desperately unhappy, my husband and I kept inflicting pain on each other. Like two hamsters in a cage, we trotted around the wheel of pretense, exhausting ourselves and going nowhere. We attended church faithfully and participated in its ministries. We read the Bible and prayed. I clung to a bad relationship because I didn't want to be alone and because I was determined to keep my wedding vow to stay with this man "for better, for worse." I lived in denial, unable to be honest even with myself about my deep hurt and our problems.

One aspect of the Bible that I admire is its honesty about human nature and human problems. We see this in many of its stories, including that of Abram (later Abraham). Abram was a liar (see Genesis 12)—and also the one through whom God promised to bless all the nations of the earth. Genesis 13 shows Abram facing the strife among his family members and realizing that they can no longer live together. Sometimes, the only healthy and life-supporting choice is separation. That doesn't take away the pain, but it gives both parties in the conflict a chance to find a better way of living.

Seeing and admitting the brokenness in a relationship can be wrenching, almost impossible. We may not want to admit that relationship choices have taken us far from the fullness of life that God wants for each of us. But divorce is not murder; divorce is a funeral for a dead relationship.

Perhaps we need a divorce ceremony in the church, a way for the community to mourn and to support those who are grieving the death of a relationship. The church still struggles with balancing support for marriage and families with support for those whose marriages end. But the epistle to the Romans says, "Weep with those who weep" (Rom. 12:15), reminding us to acknowledge the reality that believers suffer pain and encouraging us to help one another when those times come. Divorce is one of them.

Prayer

Dear God, acknowledging the pain we have suffered and inflicted is difficult. Help me to name my pain and to allow you and your people to help me carry it. I pray in the name of Christ, who came to bear our sorrows and to give us life in the face of death. Amen.

Reflection

Who has offered me a safe place to acknowledge my pain, and how can I offer that safety to others?

FRIDAY
Death throes

Read 2 Samuel 18:24-33 and Psalm 40:1-4.

[David cried,] *"O my son Absalom, my son, my son Absalom! Would I had died instead of you, O Absalom, my son!"*

—2 Samuel 18:33

The scene of David walking the wall of his palace lamenting the death of his son Absalom is one of the saddest pictures in all of the Bible. David, overwhelmed by grief, cries out his son's name.

Years ago, Dr. Elisabeth Kübler-Ross did groundbreaking research about grief. She identified five stages in the process of grieving: denial, bargaining, anger, depression, and acceptance. Grief accompanies every loss, including the loss of a relationship.

David's family has been torn apart by the sin of his son Amnon and by Absalom's revenge for it. The story describes David as "very angry" (2 Sam. 13:21); in later verses he seems depressed (13:37-39); in another he bargains (14:21-24). David struggles because of his family's woundedness. The scene on the palace wall is the culmination of years of loss, pain, and bitterness. And we see that David finally admits his own pain.

No psychologically healthy person wants to experience pain. When we find ourselves in painful situations, we may also find ourselves shrinking back from admitting the depth of our pain and from examining its source. Sometimes people avoid counseling because they don't want to talk (or to talk *again*) about painful experiences.

We don't necessarily progress through the stages of grief in the order that Kübler-Ross discussed them. We may work through bargaining and anger but drift back into them or find ourselves slipping back into depression after we thought the sadness had lifted. This back-and-forth is normal.

No matter how bad a marriage may have been, facing its end opens the door to grief. At one point in my grief, I said to God, "I know that there are better days ahead, but can't I just jump from here to there and skip all the pain and struggle in between?" Though I wanted to do that, it is not possible. As a poster I once saw read, *The only way out is through.*

Then I came across a verse in scripture that helped me remember that God's work of restoring us is a process: "After you have suffered for a little while, the God of all grace, . . . will himself restore, support, strengthen, and establish you" (1 Pet. 5:10). I saw in that verse a fourfold assurance: God would hold me up when I felt weak; strengthen me through what I endured; and, with time, make me strong and finally "establish" me, restoring me to wholeness and stability. I copied that verse onto a card and put it at eye level on my refrigerator door where I could see it often. It didn't relieve the pain, but it reminded me of God's work. The verse convinced me that no matter how bad my life seemed on any given day, with God's help I would be restored to strength and happiness. I can bear witness to the truth of that statement.

Prayer

God of all comfort, help me to trust that you will restore me, strengthen me, and set me on firm footing again, especially in times when that seems too big a task even for you. Amen.

Reflection

Which stage of grief am I in today? What do I want to say to God about my feelings?

SATURDAY
The weight of failure

Read John 8:1-11.

> *God did not send the Son into the world to condemn the world, but in order that the world might be saved through him.*

> —John 3:17

In Nathaniel Hawthorne's classic novel *The Scarlet Letter*, Hester Prynne is required to wear a scarlet *A* on her clothing for the rest of her life, branding her as an adulteress for all to see. When I divorced, I felt as if I were a modern-day Hester wearing an enormous red *D* on my forehead among our Christian friends and within the church. I felt marked, exposed, and condemned.

Though divorce is saddeningly common, even our secular culture values a traditional home and family. Going beyond the civil marriage contract, we Christians say our wedding vows not just before civil authorities but before God. Yet, as a Christian who married a Christian, I was divorced. How could this have happened? We had promised to love each other until death. Instead, we had hurt each other, year after year. We had failed each other; I had failed myself—and God. This thought was almost more than I could bear.

I have never met a divorced person for whom divorce was a casual decision. People don't divorce because someone left the cap off the toothpaste or kept a crazy schedule. Those who end a marriage do so because they feel that there's no other option they can live with. The details of the pain and problems are not really that important. Every marriage has its unique problems, and every bad marriage has its array of destructive and painful ones. Divorce is a last resort.

Although divorce acknowledges failure, it does not make *me* a failure. It is does not make *you* a failure. Divorce happens because people are weak and sinful—every one of us. Romans 3:23 says "All have sinned"—not just some of us. *All* of us. Though sin plays a part in every divorce, God forgives these sins as surely as any others. As Romans also says, "There is therefore now no condemnation for those who are in Christ Jesus" (8:1). And 1 John 3:20 tells us, "Whenever our hearts condemn us . . . God is greater than our hearts." God's grace extends to us in our failures, including the failure of a marriage, and sinks deep into our heart. With time, it displaces the guilt and self-condemnation. God does not condemn us, even when we want to condemn ourselves or feel condemned by others.

Prayer

Dear God, when I feel judged by others and when I am harsh with myself, remind me of your kindness. Help me to remember that you do not ask for perfection and that you love me in my worst moments. In the name of Jesus, who refused to condemn. Amen.

Reflection

Where have I seen evidence of God's kindness? How can I show kindness to others and welcome those who are in pain?

SUNDAY
Carving the tombstone

Read Philippians 4:5-9.

Set up road markers for yourself, make yourself guideposts; consider well the highway, the road by which you went.

—Jeremiah 31:21

I love to walk in old graveyards and read tombstones, daydreaming about the people buried beneath them. It's no surprise, then, that I love Edgar Lee Masters' *Spoon River Anthology*. Published almost a hundred years ago, the book gathers supposed epitaphs from the cemetery of the fictional town Spoon River. Each epitaph is written as if spoken by the person whose grave it marks.

Thinking about words to choose for a tombstone can provide a helpful way to think about the death of a marriage. After a divorce, we have to decide what we want to remember and what we need to forget. Why would we have married a person with no redeeming qualities or tried to save a relationship that had no good in it?

Along with the problems, even bad marriages had good moments that we can and should remember. Identifying, remembering, and celebrating the good in the relationship becomes especially important if children are involved. After all, children get half their chromosomes from each parent. We help children feel good about themselves when we focus on the good traits of their parents. What drew you to your spouse? A sense of humor, a love of music, commitment to common values? We can decide to claim the good.

In thinking about what to keep, we also consider the relationships that marriages create beyond the one between wife and husband. Most of us probably want to keep ties to grand-parents and cousins. Children look for assurance that they are not alone, and maintaining ties to extended family helps meet that need. I didn't stop loving my nieces and nephews and in-laws or caring about their lives after the judge signed the divorce decree. These extended-family relationships inevitably change when divorce comes, but we can consciously claim what was good in them.

Spouses "become one" on many levels, and dissolving the ties is a process. Writing a symbolic epitaph can help us free ourselves. What would you put on the headstone for your marriage? Mine would say, "Good books, good talks, good laughs." I grieved the loss of that and much more. Naming and grieving the losses helped me realize that my marriage was over. It helped me close the door on that chapter of my life in order to move forward.

Prayer

Dear God, help me name and grieve the losses that I can see today. Be with me as I grieve others that I will realize in the future. Teach me how to be who you want me to be now that I am not married. In the name of Jesus, who in his grieving and weeping showed us that doing so is right and good. Amen.

Reflection

Write an epitaph for your marriage memorializing the good you identify in it, the losses you grieve, and the events and traits you want to remember.

WEEK 2

The Road to Freedom—Forgiving

MONDAY
Deflating the beach ball

Read Hebrews 12:14-15.

> *So Absalom lived two full years in Jerusalem, without coming into the king's presence. . . . After this Absalom got himself a chariot and horses, and fifty men to run ahead of him.*
>
> —2 Samuel 14:28; 15:1

When we push old hurts out of mind and refuse to acknowledge the problems they represent, the unresolved pain does not just sit there. On the contrary, unresolved feelings sour. Like a covered wound, they can fester. They can make us what my mother called "sick at heart"—deeply sad. They can become a "root of bitterness" (Heb. 12:15) that grows and eventually bears bitter fruit.

The Bible story of Absalom and David depicts this truth. The story (told in 2 Samuel 13–18) is an involved one. After Absalom killed his brother in revenge, Absalom was banished. But while he was in exile, the anger he harbored did not go away. In fact, when he came back to Jerusalem, his resentment had grown even stronger. He recruited an army and mounted a rebellion against his father. For us, as with Absalom, unresolved hurt and anger can become rancid and toxic, poisoning our present and our future relationships.

Many years ago I heard a statement about troubling feelings and memories that has stayed with me. Trying to ignore negative experiences is like trying to hold an inflated beach ball underwater. It can be done, but doing so takes both our hands and constant attention. If something draws our attention away from holding the ball down, what happens? It comes flying out of the water, spraying everyone nearby and often hitting an innocent bystander. In a similar way, many of us are holding down emotional beach balls filled with yesterday's hurts and bad memories. Doing so takes energy—energy that we could invest in dealing with today's challenges but must use instead to babysit the past.

We take the first step in deflating these beach balls by looking honestly at the hurt we have experienced. Sometimes this honest look requires effort; but as Jesus told his friends, the truth sets us free. (See John 8:32.) With God's help, we can take this first step on the road to freedom.

Prayer

Dear God, facing pain is tough. It seems easier just to push it away. But as the psalmist wrote, you "desire truth in the inward being" (51:6). Help me to face the pain of this severed relationship, knowing that you walk with me in this place of shadows. Amen.

Reflection

What's inside my beach ball? Whose name is on it?

TUESDAY
Loosing the chains

Read Matthew 18:23-35.

If you forgive others their trespasses, your heavenly Father will also forgive you; but if you do not forgive others, neither will your Father forgive your trespasses.

—Matthew 6:14-15

One night about a year after our divorce, my former husband called to talk over arrangements about our daughter. We settled those details, and a few sentences later I became angry, told him I did not want to talk with him, and hung up. A wise friend who was visiting overheard my words and said, "I guess you're not really free of him, are you?" When I asked what that meant, he said, "If he can make you that angry that quickly, you are not free." He was right.

The anger came, as most anger does, from unresolved hurt. My husband told me during our marriage that he did not love me, that he had not loved me when he married me, and that he was not sure he ever could love me. For the rest of the years of our marriage and after our divorce, these and other statements he made to me and about me stayed in my mind.

I had erected my own "debtors' prison," and my former husband had a permanent cell in it. I visited him each time I replayed those old, hurtful words said during our marriage. But tending a private debtors' prison imprisons us as well. My friend's comment helped me to see that hurt and disappointment were chaining me to the past. Unless I could forgive, I would remain linked to my husband in ways that limited my life.

I didn't feel loving and compassionate toward him, and I didn't really want to forgive him. But forgiving goes beyond feeling to deciding. And once we decide to try to forgive, the chains that bind us to the past begin to fall away.

When is the right time to forgive? The right time presents itself each time we recognize the past seeping into the present and contaminating today. That realization is God's invitation to forgive and become more fully free.

Prayer

O God, sometimes I'd prefer to pretend that all is well. But I ask you to help me see where and whom I need to forgive with regard to the end of this relationship. And then help me become willing to do so. Amen.

Reflection

What hurt and scars take up emotional space in my life and limit me in living today? How can I move toward forgiving?

WEDNESDAY
The power to forgive—or not

Read Luke 23:32-34 and Colossians 3:1-15.

Bear with one another and, if anyone has a complaint against another, forgive each other; just as the Lord has forgiven you, so you also must forgive.

—Colossians 3:13

People say things like, "I'm not going to forgive her until she apologizes; she has to admit that what she did was wrong," or, "I'll never forgive him; he doesn't deserve it." Such statements spring from misunderstanding the nature of forgiveness.

Forgiving does not mean that another's actions do not matter or are excusable. On the contrary, forgiving is necessary precisely because someone has done something wrong and by doing so has hurt us. Forgiving begins with acknowledging the truth, as Colossians 3 tells us to do. We are not "letting people off easy" by forgiving. Rather, we are recognizing guilt.

Forgiveness does not depend on the attitude of the wrongdoer. As the reading from Luke tells us, Jesus' example does not include waiting until people are sorry to forgive them. Jesus took the initiative in forgiving his torturers. If we wait until people say they are sorry or change their ways before we forgive them, we may remain permanently chained to them by bad feelings and painful memories. Some people will never regret what they have done or stop their harmful behavior. Many of us spent years in painful marriages hoping and praying that the other person would change—and seeing that it didn't happen. Change is really quite rare.

Forgiving is also not an act of weakness and resignation. Far from it. When we forgive, we reclaim our emotional and spiritual power. By forgiving we acknowledge that we have the right to punish but that we choose instead to let go of the hurt and to pardon the wrongdoer. We release the offender from the penalty for what she or he did. When we forgive, the other person is no longer in charge of our feelings. When we forgive, we claim the power to refuse to accept being wronged.

Forgiveness is not the same as reconciliation. Reconciliation means putting a relationship back together—and that is not always possible or wise. We can forgive a person while acknowledging that being with that person is damaging to us spiritually and emotionally or even dangerous to us physically.

Paul doesn't leave much wiggle room in what he wrote to the Colossians. We "must forgive," just as the Lord has forgiven us. He echoes Jesus' words in the Lord's Prayer: "Forgive us our sins, for we ourselves forgive everyone indebted to us" (Luke 11:4).

Forgiving is a powerful tool. Do you choose to use it?

Prayer

God of second, third, fourth, and continuing chances, I know you have forgiven me many times. Help me to choose the way of forgiveness, the way of freedom and peace. I pray in the name of Jesus, the one who readily forgave his torturers. Amen.

Reflection

What in the Bible's advice about forgiveness is hard for me to accept, and why?

THURSDAY
Examining the wounds

Read Mark 10:46-52 and Psalm 139:13-18.

> [Bartimaeus] *began to shout out and say, "Jesus, Son of David, have mercy on me!" Many sternly ordered him to be quiet.*

> —Mark 10:47-48

My mother had seven children. She didn't have the time (or the personality) to cuddle us. I suppose this could have scarred my soul and psyche—except that I had a grandma. Grandma would whisper to me, "You're my favorite. I know I'm not supposed to have favorites, but I do—and it's you." She loved me without reserve. Nothing that I have experienced or ever will experience can take away what she put in me. Her love prepared me to understand and receive the love of God.

Even deeper than human love can go, the love of God is imprinted within me—and within you. When we were being "knit . . . together in [our] mother's womb" (Ps. 139:13), God was there, shaping us, loving us. Life's hurts can cause us to forget that loving formation, and we can lose our sense of connection to the love of God within us. The process of forgiving allows us to recover awareness of that love to energize and reassure us.

Yet we sometimes hide from our hurts. We minimize them by saying, "Oh, it's nothing, really. Let's just forget about it. Don't mention it." Or, "I've had much worse done to me; this is nothing." And as the story of Bartimaeus shows us, sometimes others want us to minimize or hide our neediness and pain. They want us to get over it—whatever "it" is. When Bartimaeus calls out to Jesus, people try to silence him, as if they are embarrassed by his disturbing the visiting rabbi. But

Jesus takes notice, turns to Bartimaeus, and asks, "What do you want me to do for you?" The answer seems obvious. Bartimaeus is blind, after all, and Jesus is a healer.

But Jesus' question to Bartimaeus demonstrates the importance of naming our pain. We cannot receive healing if we will not admit our woundedness. Bartimaeus wants to "see again." Those words convey enormous loss and grief. This man was once able to see, able to work and support himself and, perhaps, a family. But he lost that. Whoever he was, that identity is gone.

When we divorce, we lose part of our identity. We may feel that we've lost all the good parts of who we were. But no matter how deep the wounds, God's love for us goes deeper. Before life wounded us, before any person wounded us by telling us we were unloved or unlovable, God placed the imprint of divine, unfailing love within us. The desire for restoration and wholeness arises from that love. Forgiving those who have hurt us restores our link to that image of God in us.

Prayer

Eternal Love, may I always remember that your love is the beginning, the middle, and the end of my identity—no matter what anyone says or does to me. Help me to embody your healing love for all those I encounter. Amen.

Reflection

What sense of uneasiness within me signals unresolved hurt? Where do I still need to forgive?

FRIDAY
Naming names

Read Matthew 5:21-24.

*When you are offering your gift at the altar, if you
remember that your brother or sister has something
against you, leave your gift there before the altar
and go; first be reconciled to your brother or sister.*

—Matthew 5:23-24

No marriage exists in a vacuum. No one knows precisely
what goes on within the privacy of a home, but there are
always signs and clues. After my husband and I divorced, our
closest friends, a couple we had spent time with from the first
days of our marriage, said to me, "We feel like we owe you an
apology. We should have done something. We saw what was
going on, and we should have said something."

I felt touched by their soul searching. I doubt that my husband and I would have related to each other differently based
on anything our friends could have said or done, and I readily
extended forgiveness. Believing they could have said or done
something probably made them feel less powerless.

Another friend listened as I wondered why my husband's
family had not been more forthright in telling me his history. My friend asked, "Would you have listened?" Of course
I would not have. And some family members felt very bitter
toward me, blaming me for the divorce and the shame I'd
brought on the family, refusing even to speak to me. One rela-
tive forbade his wife, whom I loved, to talk with me. To avoid
feeling resentful, I had to forgive what I saw as their wrongs.

I also had to forgive God. A woman whose husband had
died of a heart attack while in his forties, less than two years
before their oldest son was killed in an auto accident, said,

"Oh, I had to forgive God. Until I did I couldn't feel close to him; I couldn't pray. I couldn't do anything except yell at him. I was mad at God, and I had to forgive him." I understood. I blamed God for not protecting me. I had prayed for guidance; I had prayed for my husband and for my marriage—and God did not intervene.

Once I determined to forgive those who "should" have helped, one person remained to forgive: myself. By marrying the man I did, I made a huge mistake. I berated myself, writing in my journal with perfect hindsight about my wrong actions. Finally, I had to stop doing that.

My friend's words about not being able to pray while she was angry with God go to the heart of the issue: The most dangerous effect of not forgiving comes in what it does to us spiritually. We cannot offer our gifts freely to God if we harbor anger and resentment toward others and even toward ourselves. These feelings create a wall between us and God just as surely as they create walls between us and other people.

Prayer

O God, you know all those I want to blame for the problems in our marriage. Help me to admit my hard feelings and to forgive. You know my heart, O God, and you know the times I have blamed you for not making my life what I wanted it to be. Cleanse me of resentment and anger so I can serve you with a peaceful heart. Amen.

Reflection

Where do I still need to forgive myself for my mistakes regarding my marriage?

SATURDAY
The spiral of forgiving

Read Matthew 18:15-22.

> [Peter asked Jesus,] *"How often should I forgive? As many as seven times?" Jesus said to him, "Not seven times, but, I tell you, seventy-seven times."*
>
> —Matthew 18:21-22

"Forgive and forget," the saying goes. But those two actions don't go together. The normal human brain remembers; that's why amnesia and dementia are labeled medical problems. It is not normal to forget completely what has happened to us. So as time passes, events and people will continue to remind us of our marriage. Being troubled by past events does not mean that we have made no progress in forgiving, but it may lead us to see that we are not done with the process.

Years ago I heard a sermon about Jesus' prayer from the cross, "Father, forgive them; for they do not know what they are doing" (Luke 23:34). The speaker said that people often don't realize that what they do hurts us or how those hurts affect us. He asked us to think about the person who had hurt us most. For me that was easy: my dad. He asked us to think about the worst thing that person had done to hurt us. I thought of the physical and verbal abuse. Then he asked us to pray for that person, saying, "Father, forgive _____, for that person did not realize what he or she was doing." I prayed the prayer, feeling and understanding that God was calling me to forgive. But I sensed no change in myself.

Some time later, as I was replacing the electrical plug on my toaster, I thought, *I'm glad Dad taught us this kind of stuff. I couldn't do this if he hadn't taught me how.* That positive thought about my dad signaled a change in my feelings.

But as I moved forward, I realized that forgiving Dad's actions was not enough. The effects of those actions had limited me in many ways. His verbal abuse warped my image of myself so that I doubted my abilities; I had to forgive him for that. My troubled relationship with him made it difficult for me to interact with men in healthy ways, and I had to forgive him for that. His behavior interfered with my seeing God as a loving parent, which affected my spiritual life. I had to forgive him for that. In ways large and small, I have had to forgive him again—not for new actions but for effects of the old ones.

Forgiving a former spouse is not a straight line. Forgiving resembles a spiral. At the center of the spiral lie the hurtful actions. As we come to new spiritual awareness and see connections between past hurts and present attitudes and actions, we may have to forgive again. And farther on, as we discover other pain and scars, we may have to forgive again—as many times as it takes to be free.

Prayer

God of new beginnings, as I come to see how others' actions in the past limit me in the present, help me to open my wounds to your healing light. Help me to forgive and forgive again so that I can be whole and free. I pray in the name of Christ, the one who calls us to keep on forgiving. Amen.

Reflection

Where can I see that a single hurt has affected me in multiple ways?

SUNDAY
Are we there yet?

Read Luke 10:25-37.

> [Jesus said,] *"Love your enemies, do good to those who hate you, bless those who curse you, pray for those who abuse you."*
>
> —Luke 6:27-28

One cold January afternoon some years after my divorce, I answered my office phone to hear the voice of my former husband. Over the years, our conversations had been limited. If he called to talk with our daughter when she was not at home, he hung up without saying anything more than good-bye, if that. His bitterness and hostility toward me was nearly palpable when we had to be in the same room. So it surprised me when he asked if I had a few minutes to talk. I said yes, unprepared for what came next. He said, "I've called to ask you to forgive me." I was flabbergasted. He went on to ask me to forgive him for what he'd done to hurt me while we were married, during our divorce process, and in the years since.

After I recovered my voice, I assured him that I forgave him, that I had done so many years earlier. Then I asked what had brought him to make these statements to me. His answer was simple: He had been praying—asking forgiveness for his part in our marriage's death—when he sensed God telling him that he had not asked for *my* forgiveness—and that he needed to. He noted, "This was God at work in me."

Readiness to close the door on the past, as my former husband wanted to do that day, is one indication that we have truly forgiven. Another is the absence of bitterness, which was evident as he spoke to me kindly, honestly, and directly.

Another indication that God's work is nearing completion comes when we desire and earnestly pray for God's best for the one who has hurt us. During my marriage I had prayed for my husband out of self-interest. I wanted God to change him so we could save our marriage. In time, I came to pray for God's work to be done in his life not out of self-interest but because I wanted him to have healthy relationships.

Finally, we can know that we're near the end of the journey when we find ourselves free of inner signs of physiological stress when we have to deal with the one who hurt us. For me, that was a churning stomach. For some the sign may be a headache or a backache; for others it may be nervousness or a feeling of anxiety. You can probably identify your signs.

If we still feel some inner dis-ease, however, that is not a sign of failure. Any of these signs simply remind us that we still have work to do. And we can trust that God who has begun "a good work" in us will continue it (Phil. 1:6) for as long as it takes, until we can love freely with no strings attached.

Prayer

Healer of our brokenness, guide me as I continue the journey of forgiveness. Make me quick to forgive when others hurt me and gentle with myself when I find it hard to do. Free me of all bitterness so I can love fully, as you do. Amen.

Reflection

What situations make me aware that I still have work to do in forgiving? What helps me to see how far I've already come?

WEEK 3

....

The Buck Starts Here

MONDAY
Looking in the mirror

Read Ephesians 4:15-22 and James 1:22-26.

I say to everyone among you not to think of yourself more highly than you ought to think, but to think with sober judgment, according to the measure of faith that God has assigned.

—Romans 12:3

When my friend stated, "There's always sin in divorce," I protested that divorce is not a sin but a necessity at times. He countered, "That's not what I said. I said, 'There is always sin in divorce.'" He went on to explain that sinfulness is the root of the behaviors that lead to divorce. Of course he was right. Jesus said that Moses allowed divorce because of our hardness of heart. (See Mark 10:4-5.) I couldn't dismiss my friend's words, so I began to pray about them.

Neither my husband nor I was unfaithful, so there was no obvious innocent party or big sinner. But as I prayed, I began to remember actions and attitudes that I regretted. During premarital sessions, the pastoral counselor pointed out significant problems that we'd face during our life together. He told us that we would be wise not to marry. We disregarded his loving advice. That's arrogance, which is a sin. During the weeks leading up to the wedding, I felt plagued with serious doubts about marrying, but my pride (another sin) would not allow me to call off the wedding. As I prayed, I felt that God was telling me to do just that. That's disobedience, another sin. Three sins, and I hadn't yet considered my actions *after* we married!

In counseling during my marriage, I came to realize that whenever we decide to take responsibility for our actions and stop blaming others for whatever is wrong in our life, that is the day we truly become adults. To "grow up in every way" into Christ (Eph. 4:15), I had to admit my sin and ask God to forgive my arrogance, pride, disobedience, willfulness, and superior attitude. Nothing magic happened when I did that, but I gained a new perspective. I had made my own choices; some of them were sinful ones.

Every one of us is a sinner. Once we look honestly at how we have frustrated God's hopes for us and admit what we did to hurt the person we married, that person no longer remains the only villain.

It takes faith to be honest about our failings—faith that God loves us just as much *after* we admit our sin as *before* and faith that God is faithful and willing to "cleanse us from all unrighteousness" (1 John 1:9). Even if we broke our marriage vows to honor and be faithful, God loves us and wants to free us of our shame and regret. Living with shame and regret is crippling. God sees us accurately, as we are in our worst moments, and loves us thoroughly, just as we are.

Prayer

Dear God, open my eyes to the wrong I have done. Free me of the desire to judge others and to promote myself as if I am perfect, for you and I both know that I am not. Thank you for loving me in my imperfection and for loving my former spouse as well. Help me honor my former partner as your dearly loved child for whom Christ died. Amen.

Reflection

How did I dishonor God in the way I behaved before marriage, during it, and since? What do I need to say to God today about this behavior?

TUESDAY
Drawing boundary lines

Read Ecclesiastes 3:1-8.

> *"You shall love the Lord your God with all your heart, and with all your soul, and with all your strength, and with all your mind; and your neighbor as yourself."*

—Luke 10:27

I have often said that if I were to love my neighbor only as well as I sometimes love myself, my neighbor would be in real trouble. Sometimes I don't love myself enough to care for myself well. I don't get enough rest; I don't eat sensibly; I work too much; I take on too many activities; or I make too many commitments to others.

One night when my daughter was young, I sat on the sofa with my briefcase open, papers spread around me. She asked, "Mommy, is there ever going to be a time when you don't work at night?" Her words stopped me cold. *Was this the life I wanted for her? for myself?* I saw that I had to learn to and choose to say no—even sometimes to good events at church or to more sports and activities for my daughter—in order to be free to say yes to what really matters. As the saying goes, "No one says on their deathbed, 'I wish I had spent more time at the office.'" Relationships—including our relationship with God—are our primary life assignment.

One challenge in being single comes in balancing needs and energy with life's demands. We can hide from loneliness or pain by eating too much or exercising or working or shopping obsessively. But neglecting our social, spiritual, intellectual, or physical needs ignores the scripture's wisdom about loving God with heart and soul and mind and strength. If we have children, we may be tempted (at times even encouraged) to neglect our needs in order to care for theirs. Or we may be asked to take on responsibilities with extended family because we're single and siblings are married. But the airplane speech about putting on our own oxygen mask first applies here: We must care for ourselves in order to be healthy enough to give to others. And our spirit's needs are perhaps the easiest to ignore. Prayer and time with God are the soul's oxygen, yet we often forget that we need them to live.

Being single requires giving special attention to taking care of ourselves because no one else can make us do it. Whether we need to set limits on what we will allow the former spouse to do or say to us or on how much time we will spend away from home or at work or in any activity that drains us, God wants us to choose the life-giving options.

God invites us to feed our soul, spirit, and body; to love ourselves so that we can be strong enough to love God and others well and wisely.

Prayer

O God, there is so much to do! And I have to decide and do the work alone. Help me to love myself as you do. Help me to make wise choices, to take care of my needs so that I have the strength and patience to love others in your name. Amen.

Reflection

What am I doing to meet my spiritual, physical, social, and emotional needs? In which area do I need to be more diligent, and what will I give up to make time for myself?

WEDNESDAY
With help from my friends

Read Ecclesiastes 4:9-12 and Exodus 18:13-24.

Better are two than one. . . . For if they fall, one will lift up the other.

—Ecclesiastes 4:9-10

One of my favorite John Denver songs speaks of friends talking about life and shared beliefs, noting "how sweet it is to love someone, how right it is to care." That song captures for me the yearning to know and be known, to share our lives, to love and feel part of a group.

When my husband moved out, I struggled with living alone. I'd gone from my busy childhood home with many siblings to a college dorm to marriage. I didn't know how to be single. My church saved me. I don't know what I would have done without the support I found there. But most of the single people were older than I, and almost none of them had young children.

My pastor stopped me in the hallway one day and asked if I'd help start a group for younger singles. I no longer fit in a couples' class, and starting something fresh sounded good to me. Within a few weeks more than twenty people were gathering. We were a motley crew, but we found a place in God's house to feel at home.

Our culture likes self-made, self-sufficient people. But we don't have to slog through loss on our own, keeping a stiff upper lip. Scripture offers us these and many other pictures of people reaching out to each other in times of trouble: Mary going to Elizabeth when Mary becomes pregnant; Ruth clinging to Naomi when they both become widows; Job, whose friends come and sit with him for seven days in wordless solidarity when he loses his home and family. No matter what the world around us says, we need each other. We need someone who will listen to our story and understand. We need someone who (to paraphrase Albert Camus) knows the song in our heart and can sing it for us when our memory fails. God's people can be those singers for us—if we allow them to know us.

And sometimes we need more than friends. Sometimes we need the perspective of a dispassionate pastor or counselor to help us identify what went wrong so we don't trap ourselves again. Sometimes we need a spiritual friend to help us know how to pray—or to help us rest in the assurance that when we can't pray, the Spirit prays on our behalf. (See Romans 8:26.) Sometimes we need someone to listen to us and take the load off family and friends who are also dealing with the pain of our divorce. Always we need legal help to navigate the choices and pitfalls we face.

Reaching out for help does not indicate weakness. It's a sign of intelligence and a sign of trust in God. The place to begin finding help is with God's people.

Prayer

Dear God, lead me to those who can help me honor you in how I deal with the end of my marriage. When I need more help than friends or family can give, guide me to wise counselors. Amen.

Reflection

What kind of help do I need in order to get through what I'm facing? Who can show me where to find help?

THURSDAY
I'm the very first one

Read Psalm 126:1-6.

> *Blessed are those who mourn, for they will be comforted.*

— Matthew 5:4

Mourning does not feel like a blessed state. We mourn because we've lost something or someone precious to us. But "They will be comforted" tells us why mourning can be a blessing: We can meet God there.

How can we confirm that the Gospel writer meant that *God* will comfort us? The answer requires some understanding of how Jews speak of God. One of the Ten Commandments given to Moses was "You shall not make wrongful use of the name of the LORD your God" (Exod. 20:7). Jews so revere the name of God that they do not speak it. Instead they use phrasing that's called the "divine passive," not naming an actor when the actor is God. Jewish readers and hearers would know that "they will be comforted" meant God would be the comforter. Matthew assures us that God will comfort us when we mourn.

But how does God do this? Some people feel God's presence when they pray, read the Bible, or write in a journal. These people experience God's comfort directly. Many of us need more—which reminds me of the story about a little boy who feared the dark. When his parents tucked him in bed, they told him that he didn't have to be afraid because God was with him, in his bedroom. But one night, after listening to many entreaties, his dad came to the door. When he did, the little boy said, "Daddy, I know God is here with me, but right now I need somebody with skin on."

When it comes to being comforted, most of us need "somebody with skin on." God's love and care become real to us through people who embody God's caring presence. That's why it's critical to be with God's people as we work through losses such as divorce. We don't get together to lick one another's wounds and wallow in self-pity; we seek others who can understand what we're going through, listen without judging us, and show us God's love as we heal.

The end of my marriage led me into relationship with a group of wounded, struggling Christians who were also grieving the loss of their marriages. As I grew to know them for the gifted, "normal" people they were, I began to believe that maybe I was okay too.

Whatever our situation, we take comfort in knowing others have walked the road before us and found a good place at its end. I cannot comfort someone whose child has died; I've never had that experience. I can't reassure someone who's lost a job and can't find another one because I've never been there. But I know what it is like to lose a dream and feel that life will never be good again. The fellowship of suffering allows us to become God "with skin on" for those in pain.

Prayer

Mender of broken hearts, help me find those who are walking this road that I am on. Teach me how to receive your healing love through them, and show me how to embody your love and care for those who need you to be real to them in their time of pain. Amen.

Reflection

How do I experience God's comfort?

FRIDAY
Yours, mine, and ours

Read Colossians 3:8-15.

> *All must test their own work; then that work, rather than their neighbor's work, will become a cause for pride. For all must carry their own loads.*
>
> —Galatians 6:4-5

The 1968 movie *Yours, Mine, and Ours* tells the story of a widowed Navy officer who marries a nurse whose spouse has died. Between them they have eighteen children. Then they have another child together—the "ours" in the title. Their story examines the challenges they face. The officer is a caricature of a military man, walking through their new house with a clipboard, assigning chores and roommates, trying to run their home as he would a ship, with military precision and discipline. She is the classic free spirit who has never bothered much about order and discipline. You can see the potential conflicts.

Anna Karenina's opening line states, "Happy families are all alike; every unhappy family is unhappy in its own way." My husband and I came into our marriage with our individual wounds and needs, like every couple, and with different ideas about family, money, conflict, politics, and faith. As the years passed, our efforts to meet our own needs put us in opposition to each other. Our weaknesses and faulty ways of relating created our unique misery—the "ours" in our story.

When we look back at our marriage, we may be tempted to determine who is more to blame for its end. But fixing blame uses emotional energy while accomplishing nothing. As my friend's worldly wise seven-year-old often says, "It is what it is," and "You git what you git and don't throw a fit." Blaming someone else allows us to take the spotlight off ourselves (which is probably why we do it). God asks us to take a more productive approach. It doesn't matter who is to blame—if anyone is. It is what it is. Beyond blaming others, we look at ourselves in order to work toward a healthier future.

Prayer

Dear God, you know all about my marriage. You know what each of us did that harmed the other and weakened our relationship. Help me to let go of blaming and trying to figure out how we could have fixed the problems. Help me let go of the past and begin to look clearly at what I need to do now to make the future better. In Jesus' name. Amen.

Reflection

In two lists, one about yourself and your behaviors and one about your former spouse, note the troubled and troublesome ways of speaking and acting that caused difficulty in your marriage. In a separate list, identify the fruits of these beliefs and behaviors that are the "ours" in your history. Then, as a symbol of putting blame behind you, burn or shred the first two lists. (Keep list #3, "ours," for tomorrow's reflection.)

SATURDAY
New rules

Read John 5:1-11.

[Jesus said to the man at the pool of Bethzatha],
"Do you want to be made well?"

—John 5:6

The story of Jesus healing the lame man at the pool in Bethzatha contains a question that goes to the heart of change—or the lack of it. The man has been lame for thirty-eight years, waiting at the pool to be healed. The first person to enter the pool after an angel stirs the waters is always healed. When Jesus arrives, he asks the man a question that seems to have an obvious answer: "Do you want to be made well?" We would expect the man to respond with an immediate and enthusiastic yes. Instead he makes an excuse: "The others always get into the pool faster than I can."

"Do you want to be made well?" is a question we can ask on many levels: Of Congress: "Do you want to be made well?" Do you want to shake off self-interest and do what needs to done for our country? Of our towns: "Do you want to be made well?" Do you want to address crime and homelessness and economic decline? Of ourselves: "Do you want to be made well?" Do you want to eat wisely and exercise more? Do you want to spend time with God and be conformed to the image of Christ? And we can ask it about our relationships: Do you want to relate to others in ways that help you and them to move toward spiritual and emotional health?

We learn how to "do" life and relationships in our family of origin. For example, some families deal with conflict by ignoring it; some yell and throw things; some people give the cold shoulder or withdraw. We learn our family's ways of dealing with money, of approaching work and school. We learn values about our friends, about dealing with people—about everything we face.

Some of those patterns and attitudes are healthy and serve us well; others cause problems. The recovery movement has a saying, "If you do what you've always done, you'll get the results you've always gotten." Our relationships can be life-giving instead of what we experienced in marriage. If we behave differently, our relationships will be different.

Jesus encouraged the man at Bethzatha to choose health and fullness of life. And as we read a few days ago, the apostle Paul urged the Colossians to put off "the old self" (3:9) and put on the new self of kindness, compassion, humility (3:12), and forgiveness (3:13) in order to honor God. As scary and difficult as change is, Christ wants to help us replace destructive patterns such as manipulation, deceit, name-calling, and judgment with honest conversation and loving, genuine ways of speaking to and dealing with others. Changing patterns of behaving is not easy, but Christ lovingly asks us, "Do you want to be made well?"

Prayer

God of truth, help me see how my actions and responses contribute to problems in my relationships. Show me how to interact in honest, encouraging, and loving ways. Then give me the courage to live that way. Amen.

Reflection

As I look at the "ours" list from yesterday, what unhelpful or destructive patterns can I identify in my ways of relating to others? What patterns and behaviors do I need to change?

SUNDAY
Letting go

Read Romans 12:9-21.

If it is possible, so far as it depends on you, live peaceably with all.

—Romans 12:18

This verse from Romans offers great wisdom for relationships and for how we use our energy. First, it acknowledges the uncomfortable truth that we cannot always live in peace. We want to believe that we can live free of conflict. In fact, many of us have been taught to maintain superficial peace at any price—sometimes at the high cost of losing dignity, autonomy, and personal safety. God does not want us to pay that price.

Sometimes the only self-loving and life-supporting course of action comes in acknowledging that peace is not possible. This requires looking honestly at the behavior of others and of ourselves. Naming destructive behaviors is a necessary step in understanding the limits of seeking peace. We cannot change others. (We can't even change ourselves; if we could, we'd all love vegetables and exercise.) Sometimes we can only limit the damage they inflict—and we should act to do so. When we ask for wisdom, scripture tells us that God will give it. (See James 1:5.) Then we pray for courage and support to act on that wisdom.

We cannot control others. It's sometimes tough to control ourselves even when we want to. (Back to the vegetables and exercise.) Control is not an illusion; it is a delusion. We fool ourselves if we think we can control what happens in future interactions with our former spouse. That person may never want to change. But we are in charge of how we *react*.

We can ask God to help us prepare us for future interactions. When we find ourselves facing troublesome behavior, we can ask ourselves what need the troublesome person is trying to meet. With that approach, we may gain insight into the behavior while recognizing that we are not responsible for meeting everyone's needs.

We can also look for a new mental image of the person who tends to elicit unhelpful, automatic responses. If a former spouse throws tantrums, for example, we can picture that person as a two-year-old, thrashing on the floor and flailing arms and legs. Or if a former spouse is behaving foolishly, we might picture that person as a literal clown, in whiteface makeup and a silly costume, to keep ourselves from becoming angry.

The point is, we look for strategies that restrain us from acting automatically. We can also ask a friend to accompany us into difficult encounters and to help us reflect later on how we might have handled interactions differently. All these choices require that we think about what works and what does not.

We may wish that our former spouse were different or that we had not married whom we did. Acceptance requires giving up the wish that things could be different.

We have no power over the past, and so we must leave it in God's care. But we can choose how we will meet the future.

Prayer

Dear God, give me wisdom to accept what cannot be changed. Help me to avoid falling into the faulty ways of relating that got me to where I am. Help me see how I can honor you in this and all my interactions with others. Amen.

Reflection

How can I prepare to be more loving and self-controlled in future encounters?

WEEK 4

A Whole New Ball Game

MONDAY
Open hands, open hearts

Read Isaiah 43:15-21.

> *Thus says the LORD, . . . "I am about to do a new thing."*
>
> —Isaiah 43:1, 19

What do you do when you cut your finger? I wipe off the blood, clean the wound, and put on antibiotic ointment and a bandage. Then I protect the finger to make sure I don't hurt it further and cause the bleeding to start again. We naturally tend to protect our wounds and tender spots, and that applies to emotional and spiritual wounds as well as physical ones.

We know intuitively what the proverb tells us, "Above all else, guard your heart, for it is the wellspring of life" (Prov. 4:23, NIV). We want to guard our heart. Divorce or any great loss can cause us to close ourselves off, to hide in order to avoid further pain. But isolation can lead to loneliness and depression. God invites us instead to risk, to reach out to others, to become involved. This involvement does not mean looking for another spouse; we need distance on the failed relationship, time to heal and to see the lessons that failure offers (nothing isolates the essentials quite like failure) before we seek new romantic relationships.

But we still need people and purposeful activities. We need to serve others. As crazy as it may sound, the end of a relationship offers an opportunity. Unfettered by responsibilities to a spouse, we can try new things or go back to old pursuits that brought us joy before marriage. The troubles of a bad marriage can consume our energy and keep us from helping others or caring for ourselves. Just as a physical wound needs to be open to the light in order to heal, we must come out of hiding and into the light to heal our emotional wounds.

No one can say how long another person needs to nurse a wound before removing the bandage; only the wounded one knows how deep the wound is or what causes pain. No one can say how much time you need before venturing out. But just as long-hidden cuts can fester, our emotional wounds can fester if we hide them and ourselves.

God called to the chosen people, saying, "I am about to do a new thing." One great lie of the universe is that things will always be like they are today. That is never true. Whether today is good or bad, tomorrow and the future will differ because of God's work in the world and in us. God calls to us in our losses, reminding us that something new lies just ahead, pulling us toward the good that God wants for each of us.

Here's a thought to meditate on today: God is always up to something, and that something is always for our good.

Prayer

God of hope and promise, it's hard to believe I will be happy and feel whole again. Help me open my heart, my mind, and my life to the possibilities you are opening before me. Help me move into the future with open hands, ready to receive the good gifts that you are preparing for me. In the name of Jesus, who taught us to believe in your unfailing goodness. Amen.

Reflection

What energizes and renews me? How can I take a step in the next few days toward involving myself in this renewal?

TUESDAY
No crystal balls

Read Jeremiah 29:4-14.

[Jesus said,] *"I came that they may have life, and have it abundantly."*

—John 10:10

One of my all-time favorite scenes from a movie comes from *The World According to Garp* (1982), based on John Irving's book by the same name. In the scene I remember most, T S Garp and his wife (portrayed by Robin Williams and Mary Beth Hurt) stand on the lawn of a lovely, two-story colonial house they're about to buy. As they gaze at their future home, a small plane crashes into the second floor of it. Robin Williams turns and says something like, "We're taking it. The house is now disaster-proof!" He goes on to reassure his wife about their future in the home by saying that the chances of another plane ever hitting it are practically nonexistent.

In the years since I saw that movie, I have often puzzled those around me by saying after some destructive event, "Well, we [or it] are now disaster-proof." Wouldn't it be lovely if this were so? Wouldn't it be great to know that nothing bad will ever happen to us again? But life offers no crystal balls, no certainty.

Though we want guarantees, we can only settle for trust. One prime example from scripture records the story of Mary, the mother of Jesus. When the angel tells Mary that she will bear a son who will be the Messiah, she responds, "Let it be with me according to your word" (Luke 1:38). Mary has just conversed with an angel and apparently feels convinced that he is the real deal; but for me, even an angelic appearance would not have been enough. I'd have wanted something more to hang on to. Mary, however, trusts that God will do what the angel says. And for this, she is called "blessed."

What does God promise us? What can we trust God to do? God does not promise an uncluttered, unstressful life. But Jesus did say that he had come that we "may have life, and have it abundantly" (John 10:10). And the prophet Jeremiah told God's scattered, struggling people, "Surely I know the plans I have for you, says the LORD, plans for your welfare and not for harm, to give you a future with hope" (29:11).

Despite our experience thus far, we can trust that the future holds good for us and for those we love because God loves us and is "mighty to save" (Isa. 63:1).

Prayer

God of power and might, help me trust you when I'd prefer to have signed and notarized promises about what lies ahead. May I trust that your goodness will continue to permeate my life and that you will bear me along through the future. In the name of Jesus, who through his loving and healing showed us what you desire for us. Amen.

Reflection

How have I experienced God's goodness in the past, and how can this experience help me trust God for the future?

WEDNESDAY
The ticking clock

Read Isaiah 43:1-7.

The wilderness and the dry land shall be glad, the desert shall rejoice and blossom; like the crocus it shall blossom abundantly, and rejoice with joy and singing.

—Isaiah 35:1-2

A few years after my divorce, my daughter came to me dressed in one of her princess costumes, carrying a dowel rod with a glittery paper star taped to its end. She said to me, "I am your fairy godmother. I can make you anybody you want to be." Touching her "wand" to my shoulder, she asked, "Who do you want to be?"

I put down the book I was reading and considered her question. After some moments, during which I filtered a number of possibilities, to my amazement I realized that I could not think of anyone I'd rather be than me. No one could have been more surprised than I was. I had limped away from my marriage, barely functioning, sure that happiness was a thing of the past.

My daughter's playful fantasy caused me to see that somehow, beyond my awareness and deep within me, over time God had been working to bring healing. One of my favorite quotes about living comes from poet Rainer Maria Rilke in *Letters to a Young Poet*. He urges the recipient of his letters to "love the questions themselves" and to "live" them. Then, Rilke assures him, someday far down the road, he will find that he has "live[d his] way into the answer."

God is in the business of restoration. Joel 2:25-26 says, "I will repay you for the years the locusts have eaten. . . . You will have plenty to eat, until you are full, and you will praise the name of the LORD your God, who has worked wonders for you; never again will my people be shamed" (NIV). The story of Israel is the story of a God who relentlessly reaches out to people who wander away and who at times willfully turn away from the path that leads to life. Over and over, the Old Testament prophets tell us that God never gives up on us.

Whatever we feel about ourselves on any given day, each day God names us beloved children of infinite worth. God continually and eternally works to restore the beloved child within us, healing the bruises and losses that life hands out. Time and God are on our side.

The work may be slow; we may feel frustrated at its pace, but God is at work. We can trust that the one who made us also *remakes* us. A day will come when someone asks you a question or speaks a phrase that causes you to realize how far you have come. Then you will know that you don't need a fairy godmother; you have Someone far more real and reliable on your side—God, the restoration specialist.

Prayer

Loving God, help me to see how you have been at work in my life over the time before my marriage, during it, and since it ended. Help me believe that your work of shaping me is real and ongoing. I trust that the abundant life Jesus spoke of is still your will and your goal for me and for those I love. In the name of Jesus the healer I pray. Amen.

Reflection

How have I changed for the better because of this struggle in my life? What positive things have I learned?

THURSDAY
Old friends, new friends

Read 1 Corinthians 7:25-40.

Let each of you lead the life that the Lord has assigned, to which God called you. . . . Those who marry will experience distress in this life.

—1 Corinthians 7:17, 28

After I divorced, my relationships changed. Some ended. The truth is, people relate to us differently once we divorce. Parents may begin to hover, trying to give advice and steer our lives. Married friends, especially close friends, may struggle to figure out how to connect with us as singles. People make assumptions and may have preformed ideas about those who divorce.

One day as a longtime friend and I ate lunch together, I commented that I liked her husband. Pausing with her sandwich halfway to her mouth, she said, "That's nice. Stay away from my husband."

Thinking I'd misunderstood, I asked, "What?"

The colleague repeated, slowly and with a sweet smile, pausing between the words, "I said, 'Stay . . . away . . . from . . . my . . . husband.'" I was the same person that day that I'd been in all the months and years we'd known each other. But suddenly she felt the need to warn me away from her husband. Most people are not as blunt or as outspoken as my friend, but they may shy away from us. Some even act as if divorce may be contagious—and they don't want the disease.

But another reality comes to the fore: Those who truly care about us will see our pain and stand with us.

And we will find new friends. Before I was divorced, divorced people and their struggles were invisible to me. Once I divorced, I found a new community of other believers who, like me, knew the pain of failure and acknowledged their need for help. A small group of divorced people in my church became the ones I could call when I needed to talk or needed someone to stay with my sick child or to help me when my car wouldn't start. And I did the same for them. In the years since then, those people and others like them have shown me by their actions that I don't have to be perfect to be loved.

I learned from experience what Paul said to the Corinthians: those who marry face struggles. And those who remain single also face struggles. Being married *or* being single is tough; we only get to choose which kind of tough. Some of us are called to be single. We feel fulfilled and happy as single adults and have no desire to marry. I fall into that category. The time after divorce offers opportunity to test whether singleness is God's call.

One great gift of my divorce is coming to understand this: God's grace goes deeper than our failures, and each one of us is loved and valued by God just as we are, single or married.

Prayer

Loving God, help me understand that fear and past experiences may cause some people to step back from me. Help me see that they don't intend harm; they just don't know how to be a friend in this situation. And for those who don't draw back, I give you special thanks. Amen.

Reflection

Is being single God's call for me? Do I see singleness as an opportunity or a burden?

FRIDAY
Replacing old patterns

Read Exodus 20:8-11.

This is the day that the LORD has made; let us rejoice and be glad in it.

—Psalm 118:24

The word *holiday* comes from the words *holy day*. For many centuries before five-day work weeks and vacations, ordinary people did not have days off—except for the holy days of the church year. These sabbaths and feast days were times of rest and renewal. In contrast, our modern ways of celebrating are not always life-giving. Think of the often-exhausting bustle and pressure leading up to Christmas. Family conflict about how and where to celebrate holidays is common, even expected.

Once I divorced, I realized that holidays would—and could—be different. My husband and I had made Thanksgiving a time to invite people into our home. So I decided that my daughter and I would go somewhere the first Thanksgiving after the divorce. But travel isn't necessary. Maybe you've always wanted to volunteer at a homeless shelter on Thanksgiving. Such programs always need volunteers. Christmas offers many opportunities—perhaps joining an Advent study group, being part of a special choir, or helping with a toy program for disadvantaged children. Making a new plan for holidays in the first year of being single again is wise.

Everyday patterns can offer a bigger challenge than once-a-year occasions. Just walking into church emphasized the painful fact that I was alone. Like many newly divorced people, I paused at the door many Sunday mornings. Some people decide that going in will be too difficult and so don't go in at all—at the very time they need both the support of the faith community and the balm of being in God's presence. And some of them never return. Arranging to sit with a family or a single friend or visiting a new church that has a singles program is an alternative.

Taking part in church activities alone is just one hurdle. Missing familiar activities such as Friday pizza dinner or Sunday night popcorn and a movie or cycling on weekends can bring pain. But we can adopt or create new patterns. For example, single parents with children could gather with another family every week. Finding new rituals can become an adventure, perhaps trying a new way of exercising or serving in the community. Joining others from the church or workplace can build community and create new memories.

Patterns provide comfort; losing predictability can be unsettling. But every practice that is now a pattern was once a new undertaking. We can consciously create new patterns that give us rest and renewal. God created the sabbath for us as an act of love, and we love ourselves by searching for life-giving ways of living as single people.

Prayer

Dear God, guide me to fresh ways of living. Help me to form new patterns that nurture my hope and sustain me. Teach me how to affirm sabbath as a way of loving myself and honoring you. In the name of Jesus, who built a supportive community around him to help him do your work. Amen.

Reflection

How can I prepare to celebrate upcoming holidays and special occasions in new ways? What small rituals do I need to replace, and what are some possibilities for doing so?

SATURDAY
New dreams

Read Psalm 27:1-8.

*Delight yourself in the LORD and he will give you
the desires of your heart.*

—Psalm 37:4, NIV

When I was a senior in college, our student-body president said in an assembly, "I want to tell you about a guy I used to know." He described an awkward, unsure, shy boy who went through his junior- and senior-high-school years as a wallflower. The boy, a fervent Christian, was nearly invisible, unable to speak about his faith publicly. Then, surprising us all, he said, "I was that boy."

But "that boy" felt God nudging him to become more forceful, to become someone who made a difference in others' lives. His college choice lay far from home, and he decided that God was giving him an opportunity to change. From his first day on campus, he made himself the first to speak in encounters, greeting everyone in a friendly, confident way. He spoke up in discussions and projected a happy, self-confident image. He had to pray continually for courage, feeling like an imposter at first. Just a few weeks into the school year, he decided to run for president of the class—and won. Gradually, the new ways of relating to others became natural for him. Over the next four years he emerged as an effective leader, never telling anyone about his transformation until the day he made the speech I've summarized here.

Starting over after a marriage ends gives us the opportunity to take similar action, to have a "do-over." As you examine yourself, what talents do you see that have not been nurtured? What future possibilities present themselves? Maybe, like me, in trying to save your marriage you set aside cherished dreams either because they didn't fit with the ideas you adopted as a couple or simply because you had no energy for them. Maybe looking back on your marriage you find yourself envisioning a different future. Perhaps you're considering pursuing an interest that you've always wanted to try but did not.

Some months after my divorce, I came across a canvas tote bag bearing the message "The best is yet to be." I bought it for a newly divorced friend as an act of faith for both of us. After my divorce I had thought that the best was behind me; but as time passed, I came to see clearly that the life I lived while married was definitely not the best God had for me. God had good plans for both my friend and me, and the tote bag served to remind us of that truth.

Belief in God's goodness pulls us into the future. God places dreams in our heart and helps us make them come true. Whatever the future holds, God will be there. God wants the best for each of us. God wants the best for you.

Prayer

Dear God, I wish I could see into the future. But I know that is not possible. Help me instead to look to you in trust. As ideas and possibilities emerge, help me recognize the ones that are your dreams for me. Give me hope and courage to pursue them. I pray in the name of Jesus, the Christ. Amen.

Reflection

What am I glad to have left behind? What new things do I want to try as a single person?

SUNDAY
God, the ultimate recycler

Read 2 Corinthians 1:3-5.

> *[God] comforts us in all our troubles, so that we can comfort those in any trouble with the comfort we ourselves receive from God.*
>
> —2 Corinthians 1:4, NIV

Years ago I went through family week at a drug-and-alcohol rehab center. This time is meant to help those closest to the one in treatment prepare for what they will face when intensive treatment ends. The peer counselors are family members of addicts who have walked the road themselves. As I chatted with one of them that week, he said, "Some day you'll look back on all this and be grateful for it."

It's been over twenty years, and I'm not grateful yet. How could anyone ever be grateful for what addiction brings? But I understand what the counselor meant, in principle. Even the worst experiences of our lives can teach us. But the failure of my marriage marks one of the lowest points in my life, and it isn't an event for which I'm grateful.

On the other hand, it has changed me. Before my marriage ended I never noticed divorced people or appreciated their pain. Caring for people requires a sense of connection to them. For example, because of my work with an international magazine, I have friends all around the world, and I listen to international news differently than I once did. When a colleague told me about the bombing in central Oslo, Norway, a few years ago, I went immediately to my computer to send a message to friends who worked near the bomb site. When tsunamis hit Sri Lanka several years ago and then Japan two years ago, specific faces of friends there came to mind. The connection I feel to these people makes what happens in faraway places real and important to me.

Divorce was a "faraway country" that I never planned to visit. Going there has deepened my compassion, not just for divorced people but for all those suffering loss or the pain of failure. I am much less prone to judge, and I no longer expect perfection or predictability in myself or others.

God is the ultimate recycler. In God's economy, nothing in our lives—even our worst experiences—is ever wasted. The pain we suffer and the lessons we learn will be woven into the fabric of our lives in a way that brings good to us and to others. I cannot say what you will learn or how you will grow because of going through divorce, but I know that God will comfort and heal you. God will use this experience. And God will use you, so that the "comfort wherewith you . . . [are comforted] by God" can flow through you to others. Because of what we have been through, we can become those "wounded healers" that Henri Nouwen speaks of. We can become living examples of God's redeeming power and love.

Prayer

Dear God, help me to trust that you will use this experience in my life to bring good for me and for others. Give me patience, and help me to believe that you will continue to use me to bring your life and light into the world. Amen.

Reflection

Where have I seen God use difficult experiences from my past for good? How can I hold on to the hope that this will be true of what I'm going through right now?

ABOUT THE AUTHOR

MARY LOU REDDING is the former editorial director of *The Upper Room* magazine. Among her other recent writing projects is a compilation of prayers by Upper Room staff members titled *Prayers for Life's Ordinary and Extraordinary Moments* and the small-group study *The Lord's Prayer: Jesus Teaches Us to Pray.*

Since leaving full-time work with *The Upper Room* magazine, Mary Lou as begun classes in watercolor painting and returned to her longtime love of designing and sewing clothes. She enjoys traveling and spending time with her wacky and wonderful family. In addition, she continues to read and teach about personality and spirituality, to lead retreats, and to work as a spiritual director. Her first love in the spiritual life continues to be reading, studying, and teaching the Bible.